THE VESSELS OF GOD

Having Contact with the World without Contamination

By

J.O IFEOLUWA

Books may be purchased by contacting the Author at: **ifeoluwaseun80@gmail.com**

www.hadarcreations.com

Cover and interior Design: Hadar Creations
Edited by: Hadar Creations
Publisher: Hadar Creations

ISBN: 979-8-89145-658-7

Acknowledgements

Glory to God for completing the writing of this book. Thank You, Jesus, for Your grace, mercy, faithfulness and strength. I am forever grateful to You, my Saviour, Lord and Master.

This book wouldn't have been a success without the support and contributions of so many people. Here are just a few who made this work possible:

To my wife, IfeOluwa Oluwaseun Victoria, thank you for your unwavering support over the years.

To the lambs of God in our home: Amb. IfeOluwa OoreofeOluwa, Unique Mercy IfeOluwa and Versatile Alimi Mercy (our foster daughter), I appreciate you all for making the work of the ministry easier for me.

To the chairman of the Christian Association of Nigeria (CAN), Ondo West Local Government Area, Rev. Olowoniyi Sunday Rotimi (PhD) and all the leaders of the five blocs and ten districts of the CAN, Ondo West Chapter, I deeply express my gratitude for your all-out support towards the outstanding success of the previous editions of the Leadership Fire Conference and your meaningful contributions to this year's conference (the 9th edition).

To all the members of the board of trustees of the Shekinah Voice of Emancipation (SVOE) and Global Intercessory Ministry (GIM), your labours will not be in vain.

To all the leaders and partners of the SVOE and GIM, I thank you for your doggedness and support over the years.

Sincere appreciation goes to our publisher and his unique team, Pastor Andrew Morgridge, for their selfless labours of love and absolute commitment to the SVOE and GIM since he came to minister at our crusade and ministers' conference at the Adeyemi University of Education Ondo in 2010 and counting. Thank you so much, Daddy.

Sincere appreciation also goes to Coach Oluwatosin Olajumoke Arodudu and her team at Hadar Creations, for dedicating so much time to edit, proofread and publish this book. Thank you so much for your labour of love.

To IfeOluwa Victoria Oluwaseun, Owonifa Tope Stephen, Akinsuroju Calvary Sunday, Ololade Felix, Ajibade Sunday, Ajibade Oluwabunmilomoyi Christianah, Ajayi Oluwafunmmilayo Kemisola, Ogbonnaya Ubani Sunday, Akinnibinu Blessing MoyinOluwa, Akinleminu

Oluwatobi Isaac, Olowolagba Aanuoluwapo Rebecca and Sis. Akinsehinwa Seun—my excellent and selfless editors who worked tirelessly to make sure this work came to reality—I am forever grateful.

God bless you all.

Maranatha!

Contents

Introduction

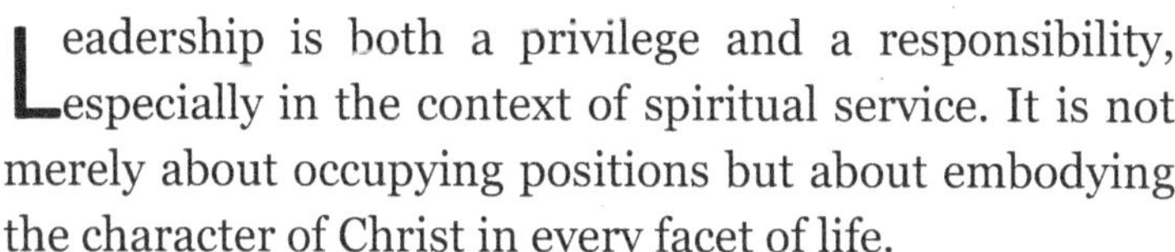

Leadership is both a privilege and a responsibility, especially in the context of spiritual service. It is not merely about occupying positions but about embodying the character of Christ in every facet of life.

The **Leadership Fire Conference** is an annual, non-denominational gathering for the ministers of God, church workers and disciples of Jesus Christ. It focuses on preaching and teaching Jesus Christ in person in order to equip the vessels of God for His work. It has, for nine years, been a great platform for nurturing such leaders—vessels of God who stand untainted in a contaminated world.

This year's theme, **"The Vessels of God: Having Contact with the World without Contamination"**, challenges us to rethink our engagement with the world. How can we interact with a culture saturated with conflicting values without losing our spiritual identity? The answer lies in intentional living, where our thoughts, words and actions align with God's truth.

To navigate this tension, leaders must remember that God knows and cares about every detail of our lives (Jeremiah 1:6). His gaze is upon us not to condemn but to guide and empower us. As Elisabeth Elliot aptly said, "He who choreographs the stars in their courses is also in charge of the tiniest details of our lives." This awareness cultivates humility, reminding us that our role as leaders is not about self-exaltation but about reflecting God's glory. Leadership that impacts eternity is born out of a heart that is deeply rooted in God, constantly seeking His will in a world filled with distractions.

The vessels of God are those who dare to be different. They are dead to the 'self' in them but alive to God. They choose obedience over convenience, righteousness over compromise and service over selfish ambition. To be a vessel of honour requires continual self-purging and sanctification, as outlined in 2 Timothy 2:19-21. In a great house, there are vessels of gold and silver, but also of wood and clay—some for noble purposes and others for ignoble use. The choice to be a vessel for honour lies in our willingness to submit to God's refining process. This refining is not always comfortable, but it is necessary for those who wish to be fit for the Master's use.

Leadership, therefore, is not about charisma or eloquence but about character. It is about living a life so rooted in Christ that our presence becomes a testimony of His grace. The **Leadership Fire Conference** is a call to embrace this higher standard, to be vessels that not only hold the truth of God but pour it out into a thirsty world. This is not a task for the faint-hearted but for those willing to rise above mediocrity and live with purpose.

"Nevertheless the foundation of God standeth sure, having this seal. The Lord knoweth them that are his. And, let everyone that nameth the name of Christ depart from iniquity. But in a great house there are not only vessels of gold and of silver, but also of wood and of earth; and some to honour, and some to dishonour. If a man therefore purge himself from these, he shall be a vessel unto honour, sanctified, and meet for the master's use, and prepared unto every good work."

— 2 Timothy 2:19-21 KJV.

CHAPTER ONE

Jesus Christ Is the Focal Point

The centrality of Jesus in a believer's life cannot be overstated. Jesus is the perfect example for every believer. His life is the blueprint for overcoming the snares of sin and the world. When we fix our gaze on Him, we see more than His glory; we see the reflection of who we are called to be. This conscious alignment transforms our weaknesses into strengths, for it is not by might or power but by His Spirit working in us. True leadership in the kingdom starts with surrendering to His lordship. If you truly want to overcome yourself, sin, the world, demons and Satan, then look unto Jesus always (Hebrews 12:2).

> *"Learn much of the Lord Jesus. For every look at yourself—take ten looks at Christ!"*
> ***— Robert Murray M'Cheyne.***

During a leadership conference in Von Gbanago, Republic of Benin, in November 2023, Pastor Daodu Olusegun emphasised a vital point: "Absolute truth is in Jesus alone. Therefore, our lives must correspond to the life of Jesus daily. A minister of God should study the Bible daily to know Jesus—not for mere knowledge. When we obey the Holy Spirit, He will fill us with power daily, not once in a while."

> *"Look unto Jesus, not self. Focus on Christ, not men or things."*
> ***— J. O. IfeOluwa.***

According to John 14:12-14, if you don't do the work that Jesus Christ did, then you are doing the work of the devil that Jesus Christ came to destroy as written in 1 John 3:8 and John 10:9-10. Focusing on Christ deepens our understanding of our mission. His unwavering obedience to the Father teaches us that purpose transcends comfort or applause. It calls for sacrifice, discipline, and humility. As leaders, we must emulate His example of servant leadership, knowing that power in the kingdom is measured by how well we serve others. In the relentless pursuit of Christ, we discover that every trial is an opportunity to grow in faith and love. Therefore, to lead like Jesus, we must look to Him not occasionally but perpetually, making Him the cornerstone of all we do.

> *"The love of Christ is the terminator of flesh. The one you obey is the one you love."*
> ***— J. O. IfeOluwa.***

It is time to seek the face of God through His Son. ***"And ye shall seek me, and find me, when ye shall search for me with all your heart"*** (Jeremiah 29:13). ***"I have not departed from thy judgments: for thou hast taught me"*** (Psalm 119:102). The Scriptures cannot be broken (John 10:34-35). Jesus was quoting the Word of God in Psalm 82:6. ***"Forever, O Lord, thy word is settled in heaven"*** (Psalm 119:89). Do not change or compromise the truth of God for anything (Romans 1:25).

CHAPTER TWO

Holiness and Sanctification

The vessels of God must be holy and righteous simultaneously. Sanctification is non-negotiable. Jesus said in John 17:17, ***"Sanctify them through thy truth; thy word is truth."***

In *Experiencing the Presence of God*, on pages 483-484, Charles Finney wrote: "Search the Bible for yourselves, and you will be astonished to find how uniformly the blessing of sanctification is held up as the principal blessing promised to the world through the Messiah. The great objective of the Messiah's coming was to sanctify His people (Ephesians 5:25-27).

Perfect holiness in believers is the very objective for which the Holy Spirit is promised. The whole tenor of Scripture regarding the Holy Spirit proves this. All the commands to be holy, along with the promises, the prophecies, the blessings, the judgments and the duties of religion, are means that the Holy Spirit employs for sanctifying the church."

To be holy is to intentionally separate oneself from the corruption of the world while remaining engaged in its redemption. Sanctification begins with a renewed mind, where thoughts are aligned with God's truth and His Spirit refines our actions and attitudes. This transformation requires daily surrender, where the believer allows God's Word to penetrate and purify their innermost being. Holiness, though challenging, is liberating. It frees us from the grip of sin, making us vessels fit for God's use.

Sanctification is a journey rather than a destination. As we grow in our walk with God, we understand that holiness is not about perfection but progression. Each step toward righteousness shapes our character and deepens our intimacy with God. On this journey, the Holy Spirit acts as our guide, convicting us of sin, revealing the richness of God's promises and empowering us to live victoriously. The call to holiness is a call to reflect God's image in a broken world, demonstrating that purity and power can coexist in a life surrendered to Him.

CHAPTER THREE

The Role of Discipline and Training

Discipline is the foundation upon which great leaders are built. Like a tree's roots burrowing deep into the earth, discipline anchors us amidst life's uncertainties. It calls us to consistent prayer, diligent study and a lifestyle of obedience. Training, on the other hand, refines these disciplines, moulding us into effective vessels for God's purposes. Through discipline, a leader learns to master themselves; through training, they gain the skills to lead others. Together, they are indispensable tools for any servant of God who seeks to make an impact.

> *"He who lives without discipline*
> *dies without honour."*
> ***— Icelandic Proverb.***

Training is essential for effective leadership in the body of Christ. It takes discipline to embrace training. An indefatigable leader should be a competent teacher, a great preacher, a seasoned trainer, a prominent researcher, and a quintessential man or woman of virtue with a strong commitment to continuous learning. He or she must be a paragon of faithfulness and possess a sonorous and mellifluous voice.

> *"We don't rise to the level of our expectations; we fall to the level of our training."*
> ***— Archilochus.***

Training also cultivates humility, as it forces us to acknowledge that there is always more to learn. Leaders who embrace lifelong learning are better equipped to handle the complexities of ministry and life. Discipline and training go hand in hand, like the relationship between a coach and an athlete. Just as an athlete undergoes rigorous preparation to compete at the highest level, so must spiritual leaders embrace the processes that equip them for kingdom work. This preparation ensures that when challenges arise, they do not falter but thrive under pressure.

CHAPTER FOUR

Faithfulness and Surrender

Faithfulness begins where convenience ends. To remain faithful is to choose obedience even when it costs us dearly. It is a quiet but profound declaration of love to God, as demonstrated by Christ's unwavering commitment to the Father's will. Faithfulness is also a measure of integrity; it tests our consistency in fulfilling our promises to God and man. When a leader remains faithful in little things, they are entrusted with greater responsibilities, becoming vessels of honour in God's hands.

> *"Faithfulness in little things is a big thing."*
> ***— John Chrysostom.***

Jesus taught in John 14:23: ***"If a man loves me, he will keep my words: and my Father will love him, and we will come unto him, and make our abode with him."*** Simply put, we must surrender to the impeccable Word of God if we want to be useful vessels of God in this end-time. To do this, we must be given to intentional, concerted and continuous discipleship training. I hope you are allowing the Holy Spirit to teach you as a leader.

> *"The best preparation for worship is not rehearsal, but surrender."*
> ***— A. W. Tozer.***

Surrender is the bedrock of faithfulness. To surrender is to lay down our will, ambitions and fears at the feet of Jesus, trusting Him to work all things for our good. This act of submission allows God to shape us according to His purpose, freeing us from the burden of self-reliance. Surrender is not weakness; it is an act of courage that allows God's strength to manifest in our lives. As leaders, we must learn to surrender daily, for it is in yielding to His plans that we find the freedom and power to fulfil our divine assignments.

> *"If you want to overcome the whole world, overcome yourself."*
> ***— Fyodor Dostoevsky.***

You must surrender to God like Christ did: ***"Not My will but Yours be done!"*** That is, we must be faithful to the infallible Word of God. We must be faithful to our callings and our Caller: the Lord Jesus Christ. It is compulsory for us to study like never before if we desire to know and obey the will of God (Matthew 7:21-23).

CHAPTER FIVE

The Effectiveness of Prayer

To be powerful vessels of God in end-time, we must be men and women of prayer who pray without ceasing (1 Thessalonians 5:16-18). It is the lifeline of a believer, connecting us to the heart of God and aligning our will with His. It is not a ritual but a relationship, a space where we can pour out our hearts, seek wisdom and receive strength.

> *"Pray and read, read and pray; for a little from God is better than a great deal from men."*
> ***— John Bunyan.***

Effective prayer requires faith and intentionality; it is not measured by length but by the depth of communion with God. In prayer, we are transformed, gaining insight and clarity to navigate life's complexities. It empowers us to fight spiritual battles, intercede for others, and claim the promises of God over our lives.

> *"God never gives us discernment in order that we may criticize, but that we may intercede."*
> ***— Oswald Chamber***

Prayer and reading (studying and meditation) must run concurrently. Prayer is a powerful force that precedes revival. Never forget that we are labouring for unity, oneness of the body of Christ, revival and the second coming of Jesus Christ in the Leadership Fire Conference.

> *"Prayers are deathless. They outlive the lives of those who uttered them."*
> ***— E. M. Bounds.***

Prayer cultivates patience and dependence on God. It teaches us that His timing is perfect and His plans are good, even when they differ from our expectations. A prayerful leader carries an aura of peace and purpose, knowing that their steps are directed by God.

> *"Not to be in fiery earnest about the things of heaven is not to be about them at all. The fiery souls are the ones that win in the heavenly fight. Nothing short of red hot can keep the glow of heaven in these chilly times. We must grasp the live coal and covet the consuming flame."*
> ***— E. M. Bounds.***

Corporate prayers can ignite revivals, while private prayers strengthen personal resolve. Leaders who pray effectively understand that their influence is not built in public but in the quiet moments spent before God. Thus, prayer is both a shield and a sword, equipping us to lead with wisdom, grace, and power.

> *"Without private intimacy, there is no public ministry. Private prayer is what empowers public preaching!"*
> ***— Alex Garrett.***

A ministry without prayer is absolute noisemaking! It is time to intercede for one another, not to criticize one another please.

> *"He who would preach powerfully must pray effectively."*
> ***— Oswald J. Smith.***

CHAPTER SIX

The Value of Studying

A 72-year-old bookseller in Rabat, Morocco—named Mohamed Aziz—habitually reads for about 6-8 hours daily. He has read over 5,000 books in French, Arabic and English. He said, "Those who can't read don't steal books, and those who can aren't thieves." If the 72-year-old can study for six hours per day, I challenge you as a leader to study for the minimum of 60 minutes (one hour) daily to grow in knowledge. Put differently, be totally committed to reading and studying as an excellent leader.

> *"Study hard, for the well is deep and our brains are shallow."*
> ***— Richard Baxter.***

Studying is the gateway to wisdom, enabling leaders to draw from the well of knowledge and apply it effectively. A studious leader is like a sculptor with well-honed tools, shaping ideas and solving problems with precision. Reading opens our minds to diverse perspectives, deepens our understanding of God's Word and sharpens our ability to communicate effectively. When we study the Scriptures, we are not merely gathering information but transforming our minds to reflect God's thoughts. This transformation equips us to teach, inspire and lead others more effectively.

> *"There is nothing new under the sun, and that is the reason why books are your cheapest source of learning."*
> ***— Grace Ngozi Onyebuolise.***

Additionally, studying fosters humility and curiosity. It reminds us that there is always more to learn and that even the most seasoned leader can benefit from fresh insights. The pursuit of knowledge should not be seen as a chore but as an act of worship, acknowledging God's gift of intellect. Leaders who prioritize study become reservoirs of wisdom, prepared to handle challenges with discernment. In a world brimming with misinformation, studying equips us to distinguish truth from falsehood, ensuring that our decisions are grounded in integrity and understanding.

> *"Those who keep learning will keep rising in life."*
> ***— Charlie Munger.***

Do you want to rise and excel in life? Then cherish reading and studying.

CHAPTER SEVEN

African Literature and the Need for Change

Many of the exploits of African heroes of faith were not properly documented because we undervalued reading, studying and documentation. For instance, the daring exploits of Apostle Joseph Ayo Babalola were poorly documented compared to the well-preserved accounts of revivalists from the West.

> *"Books give wings to the mind."*
> ***– Anonymous.***

Besides, African literature is a treasure trove of stories, wisdom and history, yet it often remains overshadowed by Western narratives. As leaders, we have a responsibility to champion our heritage by documenting our experiences and inspiring future generations. The richness of African culture, faith and resilience can serve as a beacon of hope and identity in a globalized world. By writing, reading and promoting African literature, we reclaim our voice and assert our place in history. Leaders who embrace this cause do not only preserve their legacy but also inspire others to take pride in their roots.

> *"All great leaders are well-read."*
> ***— Success Bible.***

Fostering a culture of literature among African children is likewise essential for shaping a literate and informed generation. Schools, churches and families must collaborate to cultivate a love for reading and storytelling. Investing in local authors and creating platforms for their work to flourish, for instance, can bridge the gap in representation within global literary spaces. Change begins when leaders recognise the power of words to influence minds and hearts

Therefore, I urge Africans, especially leaders, to read and study more and encourage our children to become voracious readers and perpetual learners. Let us embrace the challenge of redefining narratives and ensuring that the stories of African faith and excellence are told and celebrated. That brings us to the history of the English literature.

CHAPTER EIGHT

History of English Literature

The history of English literature serves as a window into the evolution of human thought and creativity. From the raw, poetic beauty of Old English to the modern-day diversity of voices, each period reflects the socio-political and spiritual currents of its time. For African leaders, understanding this history is not about adopting a foreign culture but about appreciating the universality of storytelling and the power of words to shape societies. English literature offers valuable lessons on how to adapt to change, innovate within tradition and document experiences with authenticity.

Now, to understand where we were coming from and where we are presently, study the brief history of the English literature below:

1. The Anglo-Saxon/The Old English Period (450–1050)
2. The Anglo-Norman Period (1066–1350)

3. The Age of Chaucer (1350–1400)
4. The Age of Elizabeth (1550–1620)
5. The Puritan Age (1620–1660)
6. The Restoration Period (1660–1700)
7. The Eighteenth Century/The Augustan Literature (1700–1800)
8. The Age of Romanticism/The Second Creative Period (1800–1850)
9. The Victorian Age (1850–1900)
10. Twentieth Century Literature/The Modern Age (1900–1970)
11. The Post-Modern Period (1970–Present)

The glaring absence of African voices in these historical periods challenges us to contribute meaningfully to global literature. The lack of representation is not due to a lack of talent but a failure to prioritize documentation. When African writers and leaders study the trajectory of English literature, they can identify strategies for creating enduring works. It is time for a renaissance in African writing, where our stories are not only told but also celebrated for their depth and richness.

CHAPTER NINE

Development and Periods of English Literature

The periods of English literature showcase the adaptability and resilience of storytelling. From the simplicity of old English to the complexities of the modern and post-modern periods, each era represents a response to its unique challenges. For leaders, these transitions highlight the importance of evolving with the times while maintaining the core essence of truth. Understanding these periods enables us to appreciate the craftsmanship behind timeless works and encourages us to pursue excellence in our creative endeavours.

The development of English literature spans a long history, enriched by the works of many great authors and poets. Based on the style and nature of their writings, the periods can be classified as follows:

1. Old English Period (450–1066)

2. Middle English Period (1066–1500)

3. The Renaissance (1500–1660)
    a. The Elizabethan Period (1558–1603)
    b. The Jacobean Age (1603–1625)
    c. The Caroline Age (1625–1649)
    d. The Commonwealth Period (1649–1660)
4. The Neoclassical Period (1660–1798)
    a. The Restoration Period (1660–1700)
    b. The Augustan Age/The Age of Pope (1700–1745)
    c. The Age of Sensibility/The Age of Johnson (1745–1798)
5. The Romantic Period (1798–1832)
6. The Victorian Period (1832–1901)
7. The Modern Period (1901–1939)
8. The Post-Modern Period (1939–Present)

Again, notice how African names are entirely missing from these periods of English literature. This highlights the urgency for Africans to contribute more to literature. We must change the narrative. Africans must study to show themselves approved both to God and to their generation (2 Timothy 2:15). This is one of the reasons why I write this book against tight schedules.

> *"A pastor must have the mind of a scholar, the heart of a child and the skin of a rhinoceros."*
> ***— Charles Spurgeon.***

As we study these periods, we arc reminded of the need to create distinct African literary periods. Documenting our journeys, struggles and triumphs can carve out a place in the annals of literary history.

CHAPTER TEN

Final Words

Leadership begins with a commitment to growth, and growth requires intentionality. The call to read, study and document is not just for personal development but for the benefit of future generations. As leaders, we are custodians of knowledge, responsible for preserving and passing it on. This requires discipline and a vision that transcends immediate rewards. When we prioritize study, we dismantle ignorance and build a foundation of wisdom that can weather any storm.

Always remember that study is the destroyer of ignorance, and every leader must be studious. In other words, we must prioritize reading, studying and documenting. These are the tools that will empower us to reshape our narrative and preserve our legacy. ***"Then opened he their understanding, that they might understand the scriptures"*** (Luke 24:45).

Ultimately, the journey of leadership is not about titles or accolades but about influence and legacy. Let us be remembered as leaders who valued learning, who pursued God with unwavering zeal and who inspired others to do the same. May our lives be books that others can read and find hope, courage and faith. As we embrace the challenge of leadership, may we do so with hearts fully surrendered to God, knowing that His grace is sufficient for every step of the journey.

May the Lord grant us understanding, in Jesus' name. Amen.

J. O. IfeOluwa,

A Product of Grace.

About the Author

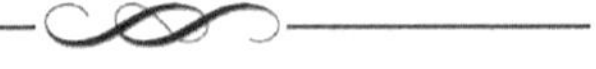

J.O. IfeOluwa is a passionate servant of God with a rich educational and spiritual background. He attended Adeyemi College of Education, Ondo, now known as Adeyemi Federal University of Education, Nigeria (2006). He furthered his studies at the Redeemed School of Mission, Ededimeji, Osun State (2013), and received international leadership training from GABIC, UK (2015). Most recently, he graduated from Christ Ekklesia Institute, Ile-Igbon, Oyo State, Nigeria, under the supervision of One Body Life, California, USA (2022).

His journey into ministry began with a life-transforming encounter with Jesus Christ in a night vision on June 19, 2004, at the Academic Block of Adeyemi College of Education. This encounter led him into full-time ministry, where he is called to serve in **Intercessory Ministry, Discipleship and Leadership Training, Missions, and Welfare Ministry**.

J.O. IfeOluwa is actively involved in cross-cultural missions, global discipleship, and leadership development. He serves as the Mission Director of **Global Missions Project (GMP)** and the Coordinator of **Shekinah Voice of Emancipation and Global Intercessory Ministry (SVOE and GIM)**. These non-denominational ministries, commissioned on July 16, 2007, are dedicated to serving the Body of Christ without discrimination, bringing glory to God.

He is happily and legally married to V.S. IfeOluwa, and together they are blessed with two biological children, OoreofeOluwa and Eri-Ife (a son and a daughter), foster children, and numerous disciples nurtured by the grace of God.

To God be all the glory!

www.ingramcontent.com/pod-product-compliance
Lightning Source LLC
LaVergne TN
LVHW091243150826
845673LV00003B/1264
* 9 7 9 8 8 9 1 4 5 6 5 8 7 *